MW01043002

On the Map

Measuring the World

Cynthia Kennedy Henzel

ABDO Publishing Company

visit us at
www.abdopublishing.com

Published by ABDO Publishing Company, 8000 West 78th Street, Edina, Minnesota 55439.

Printed in the United States.

Cover Photo: Photo Researchers
Interior Photos: Alamy p. 25; AP Images pp. 6, 8, 21, 28; Comstock p. 5; Corbis pp. 11, 14; ESRI p. 27; Getty Images p. 13; H. Andrew Johnson/Monticello/Thomas Jefferson Foundation, Inc. p. 9; iStockphoto pp. 21, 23, 29; Library of Congress p. 10; NASA p. 19; National Museum of Surveying pp. 28, 29; Photo Researchers p. 7; Smithsonian Institute p. 28; U.S. Air Force p. 15; U.S. Census p. 22; USGS p. 17

Series Coordinator: BreAnn Rumsch
Editors: Rochelle Baltzer, BreAnn Rumsch
Art Direction & Cover Design: Neil Klinepier

Library of Congress Cataloging-in-Publication Data

Henzel, Cynthia Kennedy, 1954-
Measuring the world / Cynthia Kennedy Henzel.
p. cm. -- (On the map)
Includes bibliographical references and index.
ISBN 978-1-59928-952-6
1. Cartography--Juvenile literature. 2. Geographic information systems--Juvenile literature. I. Title.

GA105.6.H48 2008
526.9--dc22

2007029204

Contents

A World of Information

To make a map, mapmakers need to know the distances between cities, across countries, and around the earth. They must know the heights of mountains and the locations of every school, road, and museum. They also need information about where people live, what they do, and what they believe. Where does all of this data come from?

Surveyors, photogrammetrists (foh-tuh-GRA-muh-trists), and **analysts** physically collect data about the earth's features, measurements, and borders. A map showing just the borders and the main features of a place is called a base map. Depending on the purpose of a map, other information can be added.

Businesses, government agencies, nonprofit groups, scientists, and individuals collect thematic data about our world. This type of data might include information about people's lives. It can also be about the **environment**, such as plant and animal populations. As you can see, there is a lot of information out there. Mapping the world is a big job!

Maps, globes, and atlases are some of the tools we use to learn about where we are and where we can go.

What Surveyors Do

In the United States, the **National Geodetic Survey (NGS)** is responsible for surveying national boundaries. NGS surveyors place permanent markers called bench marks that record the exact elevation, latitude, and longitude of locations.

Bench marks are usually concrete posts or metal disks lodged in concrete. Surveyors use bench marks as starting points for new surveys.

Surveyors measure distances, directions, angles, and elevations between points. They use mathematics to calculate the **coordinates** of new points and to measure new distances.

All of these measurements help surveyors find land, air, water, and

A permanent bench mark identifies the international border between Houlton, Maine, and Woodstock, New Brunswick, Canada.

Surveyors work with numbers every day. So, they need a college degree and a good background in mathematics.

underground boundaries. Surveyors mark these boundaries and sketch maps of important features. This information is important for legal documents.

Surveyors mark the route where a new highway will be built. They also determine the boundaries of the air above an airport. A land surveyor marks the boundaries between houses and backyards. And, a **geophysical** surveyor marks places to explore below the earth's surface for minerals or oil.

Traditional Surveying

Surveyors use special tools to determine directions, distances, and angles. A compass finds direction. Surveyors must use a very precise compass, such as a solar compass.

The Gunter's chain was an important surveying tool for many years.

To measure distance, traditional surveying was conducted using a Gunter's chain. This tool was invented by Edmund Gunter in 1620. It is a 66-foot- (20-m-) long steel chain with 100 links.

For shorter measurements, surveyors sometimes use steel tapes. However, these measuring tools are not always precise. The steel can stretch due to weather changes. And over time, steel tapes can break.

To measure angles, surveyors use a theodolite or a transit. The theodolite was invented by John Sisson in 1720. It combines a telescope, a **spirit level**, and a **vernier**. The theodolite can rotate up and down and side to side.

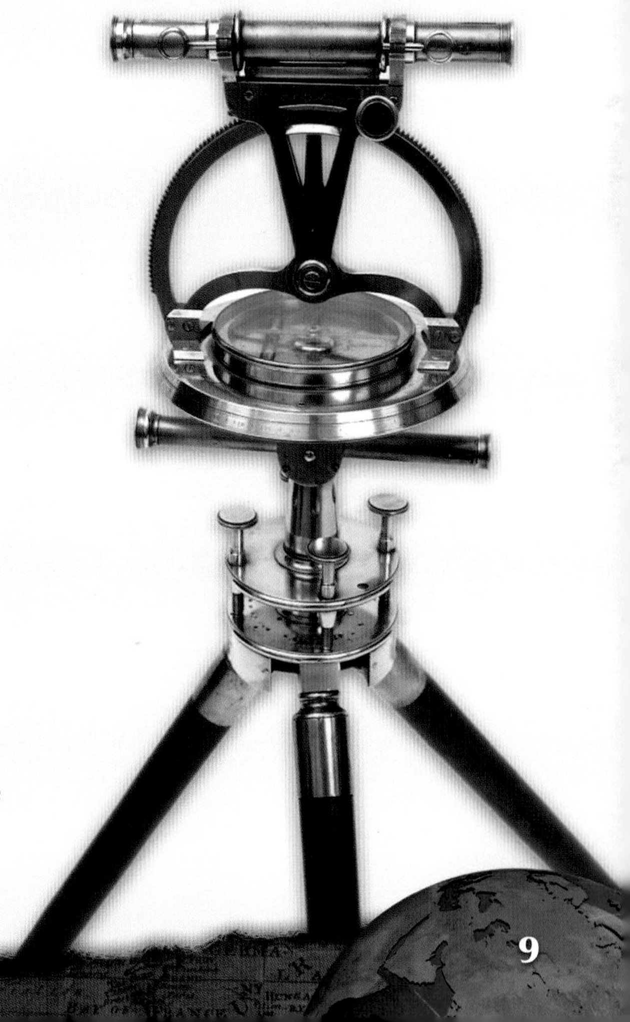

Before Thomas Jefferson served as president, he worked as a county surveyor. His theodolite remains a prized piece of American history.

The transit was invented by William J. Young in 1831. It is a theodolite that can flip over to take reverse measurements. Both the theodolite and the transit are used to sight straight lines and measure the angles between them.

The transit remained popular among surveyors well into the 1900s.

Sometimes it is difficult to measure the distance between two points. For example, surveyors may need to cross a swamp or a valley to calculate a point. However, mathematics may be used instead. Surveyors can calculate new points by using distances and angles that are easily measured.

This method is called triangulation. It uses the mathematical properties of a triangle. A triangle has three sides and three angles. If one side and two angles are known, the other three measurements can be calculated. So, surveyors can complete surveys without getting their feet wet!

Surveyors depend on triangulation when mapping rough terrain, such as a mountain range.

Triangulation

Surveyors often use triangulation to find new **coordinates**. For example, perhaps a surveyor wants to find an unknown point on a farm. The surveyor first finds a known point. This is the red barn, or Point 1.

Next, a helper takes a rod down to the white barn, or Point 2. A rod is a straight pole marked like a ruler. The surveyor sets a transit on a three-legged stand, or tripod, at Point 1. Then, he looks through the transit to locate the rod at Point 2.

The surveyor measures the distance between Point 1 and Point 2. Now he knows the length of one leg of his imaginary triangle. This is the baseline.

Another helper crosses the fields and holds a second rod at the point they want to survey. The trees are Point 3. The surveyor swivels his transit from the rod at Point 2 to the rod at Point 3. This gives him a measurement of the first angle formed from two legs of the triangle.

Next, the surveyor takes his transit to Point 2 of the triangle. He sights Point 1, then swivels the transit to Point 3 across the fields. This is the measurement of the second angle on the base of his triangle.

Now the surveyor knows the length of one side and two angles of his imaginary triangle. He can find the length of the other two sides by using mathematics. With this information, he can calculate the **coordinates** of the trees.

Modern Survey Tools

Today, surveyors use modern tools that make their jobs easier. A robotic total station combines a theodolite with an electronic distance meter (EDM) and computer software. EDMs use **infrared** signals or **microwaves** to measure distance. A robotic total station finds distances and angles and calculates new points. Then, it sends the data to computers for mapping.

The Global Positioning System (GPS) has also made surveying easier. GPS is a group of 24 **satellites** that help identify locations on Earth. The satellites orbit so that at least five are in view from most points on Earth at all times.

A GPS receiver picks up signals from the satellites. The time it takes a signal to

Robotic total stations determine the measurements of many places you visit every day, such as your school.

reach the receiver is recorded. The **satellites** have very precise **atomic clocks**. And since the signals travel at a known speed, the GPS receiver can tell how far away a satellite is. With this information, the receiver can compute its own location.

In total, there are 27 GPS satellites. Of these, 24 are always working and three are spares.

GPS has not replaced field surveyors. The system may be incorrect due to the quality of land-based equipment or atmospheric conditions. Also, it does not work as well in places where the satellite signal can be blocked, such as under trees.

A View from Above

Another method of collecting map data is **analyzing** aerial photographs. These are pictures taken from airplanes. Photogrammetrists analyze features, such as roads or buildings, on aerial photographs. Then, they create maps from this information.

Aerial photographs are not maps themselves. Airplanes sometimes fly at angles that can misrepresent the distances shown in photographs. And in the past, aerial photography did not correctly show changes in elevation.

Today, stereoscopy (stehr-ee-AHS-kuh-pee) is commonly used to study aerial photographs. This method uses an instrument called a stereoscope to help identify features on aerial photographs.

Stereoscopes use two pictures of the same scene taken from different angles. When viewed together, the images appear to have depth. So, stereoscopes make it easier for photogrammetrists to identify specific features, such as buildings or craters.

FUN FACT

Gaspard-Félix Tournachon, known as Nadar, took the first aerial photograph in 1858. He was in a hot-air balloon over the Bievre Valley in France.

An aerial view of Manhattan, New York, is highly detailed. But, satellite images do not always realistically reflect colors.

Images from Space

Satellites are also important for gathering information about the earth. They record energy from many parts of the **electromagnetic spectrum**. This includes the visual spectrum, which are the colors we can see. These satellite images look similar to photographs. Satellites also record **infrared** rays.

Satellites send data to computers in long streams of numbers. An **analyst** makes the data usable. He or she may select certain features to focus on. Then, the data is lined up with a base map.

Analysts use satellite images to map things we cannot see or easily measure. For example, satellites that record infrared rays help us map temperatures on the earth's surface.

FUN FACT

The Hubble Telescope transmits about 120 gigabytes of data each week. That's equal to about 3,600 feet (1,100 m) of books stacked end to end!

These satellites also help us map different types of plant growth. Even the health of these plants can be determined. Combinations of other energy bands show mineral deposits or the size of ice caps, for example.

Satellite images help analysts at the National Hurricane Center in Miami, Florida, monitor changes in weather systems. This way, warnings can be issued early.

Satellite data is also important for weather maps. The National Oceanic and Atmospheric Administration maintains the Geostationary Operational **Environmental** Satellites (GOES). These satellites orbit the equator at the same speed as Earth's orbit. So, they continuously monitor the same place. The National Weather Service uses images provided by GOES satellites to track storms.

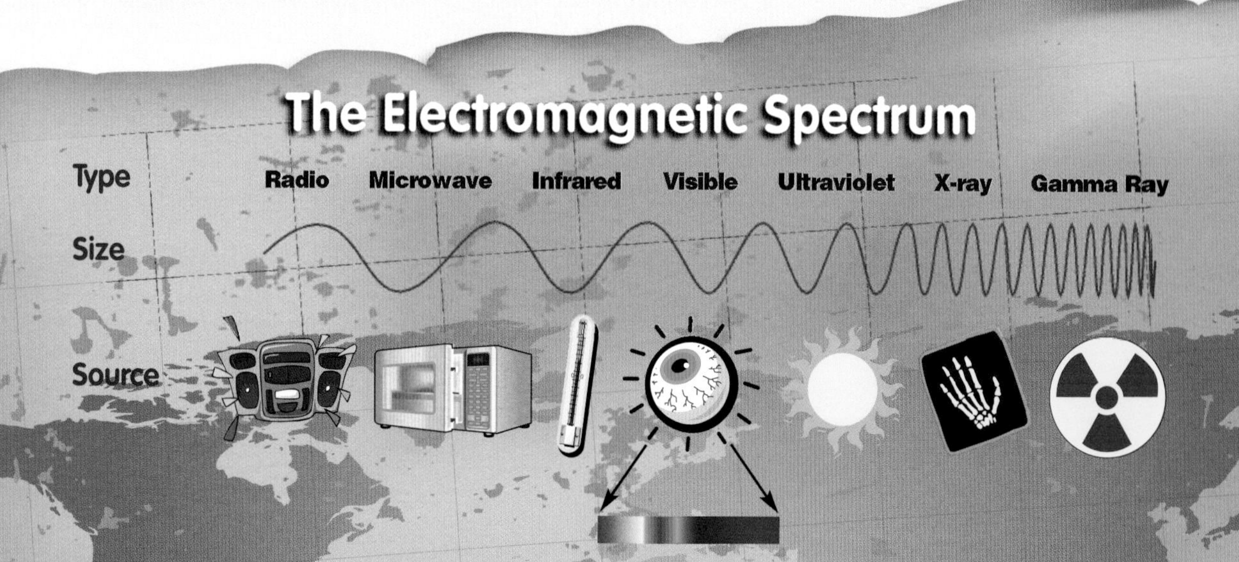

We can see only the visible light waves. To us, they look like the colors we see in a rainbow.

Thematic Data

Maps are also created with thematic data. This information usually shows **statistics** about a place. For example, a thematic map may represent the number of people, dogs, or skateboarders in California. Or, it could show the number of people in Ontario, Canada, who prefer crunchy peanut butter.

Surveys are often used to collect thematic data. But, these surveys are not completed with measuring tapes and transits. Instead, people count things or take polls to collect data. It is often impossible to count everything or to ask everyone a question. So, many surveys and polls are representative.

Polls are surveys that ask people about their beliefs, opinions, or habits. A pollster may call your family to ask what you watch on television. The answers your family gives will represent many other people. Representative data are not always precise. But, they are a good way to make an estimate.

Imagine you want to know how many people in your school wear glasses. You don't have time to visit all 100 classrooms! So, you count only the people wearing glasses in ten

Pollsters may want to know what your favorite movie is. Or, they may ask your parents which candidate they plan to vote for in an election. Answering questions like these allows people to have their opinions heard!

classrooms. You can then assume that the rest of the classrooms have about the same number of people wearing glasses.

These thematic maps show where people prefer the terms Coke, pop, and soda.

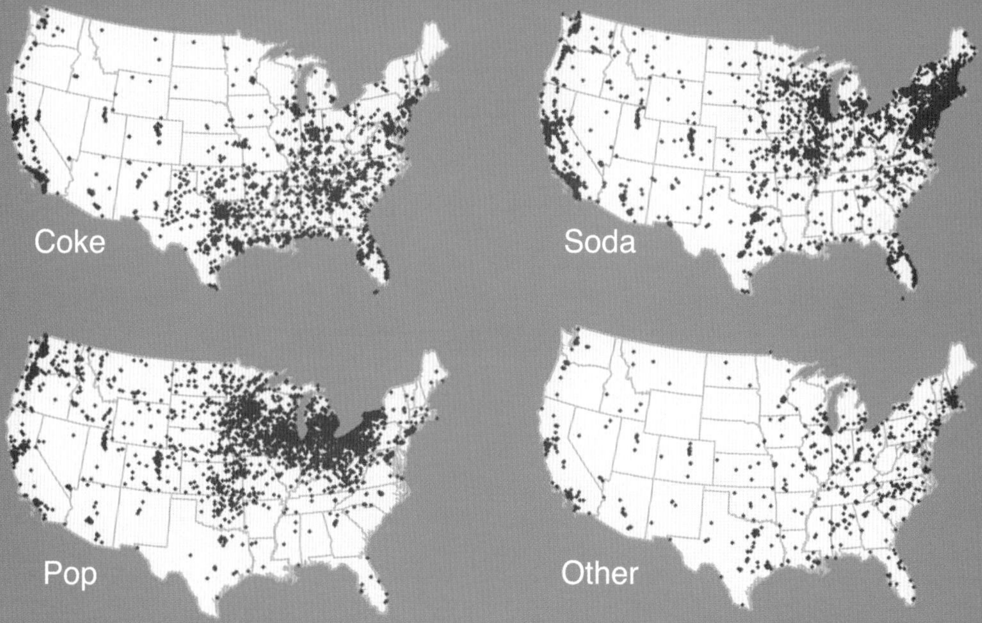

Coke

Soda

Pop

Other

A good example of thematic data collection is the U.S. Census. The law says the U.S. government must do a census every ten years. This is because the number of each state's representatives in Congress is determined by that state's population.

Census takers count the number of people. They also collect information about people's jobs, education, family size, age, and many other things.

Thematic maps often use colors to represent information. This U.S. Census Bureau map shows the average age of people in each U.S. county.

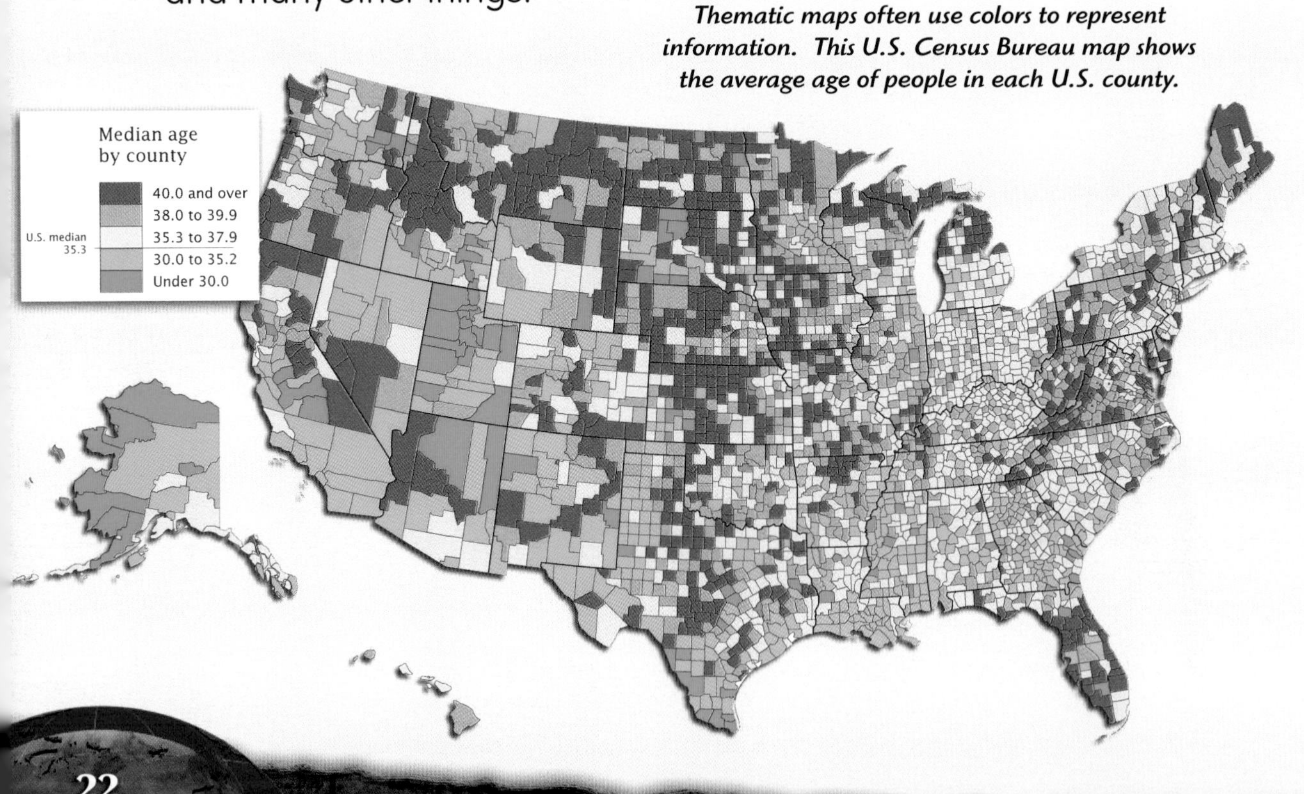

Cartographers

Surveyors, photogrammetrists, **satellites**, and pollsters collect a lot of physical and thematic data about the world. But, long rows of numbers are inconvenient to read. And, they can take a long time to understand. A cartographer's job is to make sense of these measurements by creating a map. Once the information is mapped, it is much easier to interpret.

In the past, there were few measurements of the earth. And, cartographers made maps by hand. But today, we have computers full of information about our world. We also have computer programs that make mapping faster and easier. These technologies make it more efficient for mapmakers to help us understand our rapidly changing world.

Before mapping, each piece of data must be georeferenced, or matched to a point on a map. Some of these points are called control points. They help cartographers make sure the new information lines up correctly on a base map.

Designing maps is hard work! Cartographers must make sure every measurement is precise.

After georeferencing **coordinates**, a cartographer **analyzes** the thematic data. Next, he or she chooses which items to display on the map. Then, the cartographer selects a **projection** and a **scale**. Finally, he or she creates a design that makes the map interesting and easy to understand. A good map is a picture worth a thousand numbers!

Mapping with GIS

Geographic Information Systems (GISs) are one of the most important developments in mapping technology. A GIS is a large database of information about a place.

Each type of information is called a layer. The layers may consist of reference data, such as transportation routes or the **topography** of an area. Layers may also include thematic, historical, or **satellite** data.

It is easy to think of GIS layers as many different maps of one place stacked together, like a sandwich. The layers of data are stored on a computer. So old maps can be combined, or entirely new information can be created. Mathematics reveals how the various elements work together.

A GIS specialist goes beyond the work of a surveyor or a cartographer. He or she combines information from other measurements to get new information about the world. GIS is a whole new way to measure the earth! And, it is another powerful tool to help us understand our world and plan for the future.

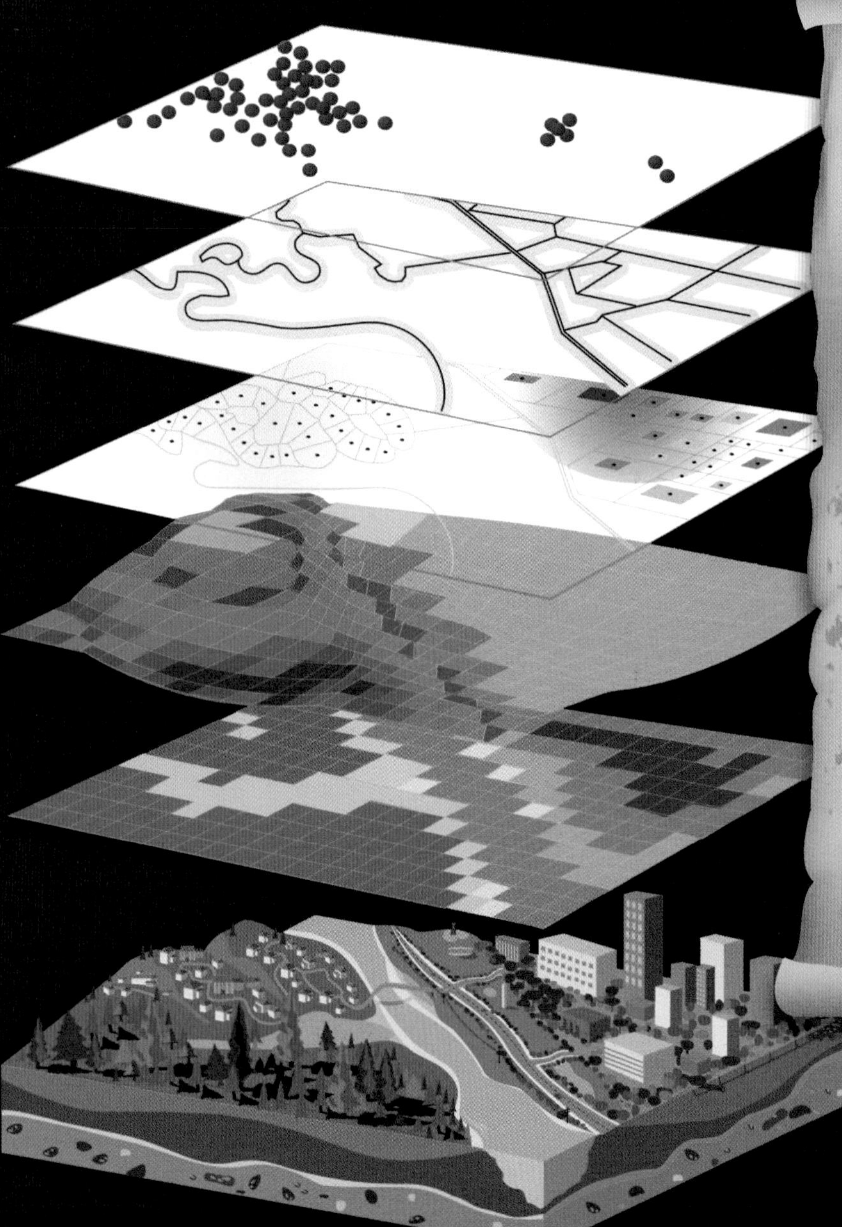

Smart Mapping

When you buy a new computer game or other item, the clerk may ask for your ZIP code. Your ZIP code and what you bought goes into a GIS with those of thousands of other buyers. Later when the company decides to build a new store, a GIS specialist studies how far people traveled to the existing store. He or she adds the average age and economic status of people living in those areas.

The GIS specialist then looks at possible locations for the new store, as well as the roads and bus lines that serve them. He or she also notes the locations of competing businesses. A GIS puts all this information together to help the company decide where to locate its new store.

An area's topography, population, and land use can all be viewed as individual layers with GIS technology.

Tools Thro

Compasses were invented long before surveyors used them. The solar compass was invented in 1835. It was such an important invention that lawmakers soon required its use on all public land surveys.

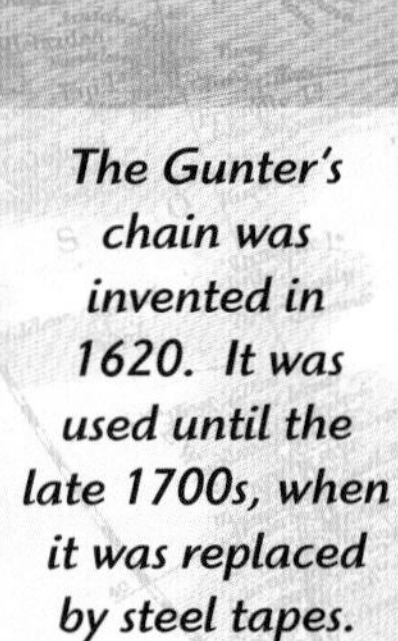

The Gunter's chain was invented in 1620. It was used until the late 1700s, when it was replaced by steel tapes.

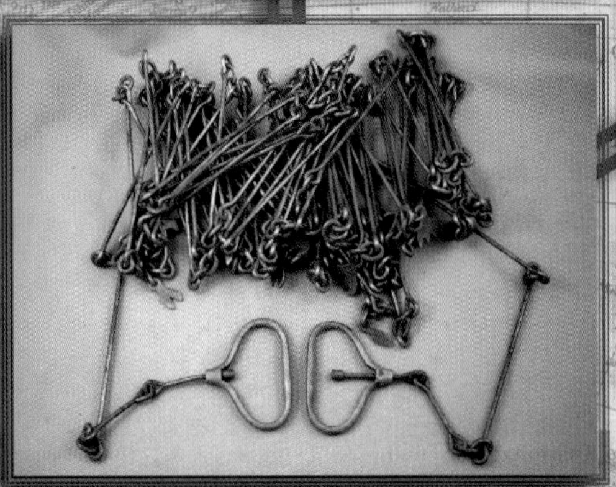

The theodolite was invented in 1720. It combines a telescope, a vernier, and a spirit level.

ugh Time

The first transit was made in 1831. It was similar to the theodolite, but it allowed the telescope to revolve. The transit continued to be used into the 1950s.

Total stations were invented in the 1980s. They combine EDM technology, an electronic theodolite, and a digital recording device.

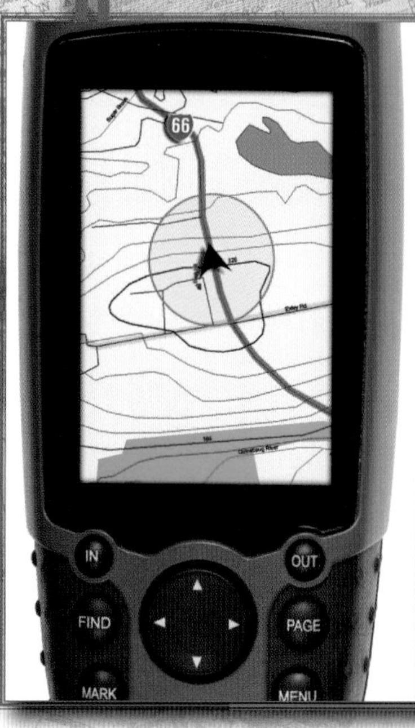

Surveyors began using GPS in 1981. Today, the Continuously Operating Reference Station (CORS) network runs more than 1,000 permanent, survey-grade GPS receivers.

Glossary

analyze - to determine the meaning of something by breaking down its parts. An analyst is a person who analyzes.

atomic clock - an extremely exact clock that uses the natural vibrations of atoms to operate.

coordinate - any of a set of numbers used to locate a point on a line or a surface.

electromagnetic spectrum - the entire range of wavelengths or frequencies of electromagnetic waves. It includes gamma rays, radio waves, and visible light.

environment - all the surroundings that affect the growth and well-being of a living thing.

geophysical - relating to the physical processes occurring in or near the earth.

infrared - a form of heated energy that resembles visible light but cannot be seen by the human eye.

microwave - a short radio wave that can be reflected and concentrated.

National Geodetic Survey (NGS) - a U.S. government agency that surveys large areas of land, making adjustments for the curve of the earth's surface.

projection - the representation, upon a flat surface, of all or part of the surface of the earth or another celestial sphere.

satellite - a manufactured object that orbits Earth.

scale - the size of a map, a drawing, or a model compared with what it represents. Also, the equally divided line on a map or a chart that indicates this relationship.

spirit level - an instrument used to find whether a surface is level, indicated by a perfectly centered air bubble in a liquid-filled glass tube.

statistic - a quantity that is calculated from a sample.

topography - the shape, height, and depth of the features of a place. A topographic map indicates these features.

vernier - a small device that measures fractions of the measurements taken by the instrument it is attached to.

Web Sites

To learn more about cartography, visit ABDO Publishing Company on the World Wide Web at **www.abdopublishing.com**. Web sites about cartography are featured on our Book Links page. These links are routinely monitored and updated to provide the most current information available.

Index

Grove K-4 Media Center